Last Kind Words

Last Kind Words

edited by

Peter Riley

Shearsman Books

First published in the United Kingdom in 2021 by
Shearsman Books Ltd
PO Box 4239
Swindon
SN3 9FN

Shearsman Books Ltd Registered Office
30–31 St. James Place, Mangotsfield, Bristol BS16 9JB
(this address not for correspondence)

www.shearsman.com

ISBN 978-1-84861-728-5

CONTENTS

LAST KIND WORDS

PREFACE, LYRICS, & NOTES

It was exactly as if these people happened to be in the room when we played the song, 'Last Kind Words', and everybody listened, and heard. I thought of asking them to say, in writing, what they had heard. Some wanted to and some didn't. There was no qualification of any kind, authorial or literary. They were in the room because of their interest in poetry and therefore, song and that was enough.

The song, 'Last Kind Words Blues', was recorded in 1930 in a makeshift studio in Grafton, Wisconsin, and issued by Paramount Records as one side of a 78rpm shellac disc with the musician's name given as " Geeshie Wiley". It's not a simple lyric. It's not about slavery, but slavery is there in it. It's about the victims of war, but then forgets about that and after verse 4 goes off into transferable formulae of the genre (floating verses) which can be shifted from song to song at the singer's wish, and therefore share a communal voice, almost always of lament in failing love. There is also a complicated and in parts disturbing story attached, which you don't have to know.

Nothing is certainly known about Geeshie (or Geechie) Wiley beyond that she was that rare thing, a female songster in the American south. She left only six recorded songs. The session at which these were recorded was shared with L.V. ("Elvie") Thomas, who probably plays second guitar on Last Kind Words and might have ben the author of the lyrics. Both were living in Kansas City at the time. 'The Ballad of Geeshie and Elvie' by John Jeremiah Sullivan in *New York Times Magazine* April 13th 2014 is a very long and fascinating account of a quest for her memory.

There have been several attempts to transcribe the lyrics of *Last Kind Words*, which are very difficult to hear in the original recording. Below is the version I sent out to the contributors, with some uncertainties and variants noted. I have removed the word "Blues" from the title on the grounds that formally the song is not a blues, and I think that at that time record companies were liable to stick the word on the end of any title as a selling point in what was called the "race" market – discs for selling to the black population.

(1)

The last kind words I heared my daddy say
Lord, the last kind words I heared my daddy say

(2)

If I die, if I die in the German war
I want you to send my body, send it to my mother, Lord
[to my mother's door

(3)

If I get killed, if I get killed, please don't bury my soul
I p'fer just leave me out, let the buzzards eat me whole

(4)

When you see me comin' look 'cross the rich man's field
If I don't bring you flour I'll bring you bolted meal

(5)

I went to the depot, I looked up at the sun
                                        [at the stars
Cried, some train don't come, there'll be some walkin' done

(6)

My mama told me, just before she died
Lord, precious daughter, don't you be so wild
                                        [so wise

(7)

The Mississippi river, you know it's deep and wide
I can stand right here, see my babe on the other side
                                        [my face
                                                [from the other side

(8)

What you do to me baby it never gets outta me
I may not see you after I cross the deep blue sea

The German war: I take this to be 1914–18, which the U.S.A. entered in 1917.

Bolted meal is, I think, coarse grained flour used for low quality bread or even animal feed.

A simple request to Google will get you the 1930 recording (The accompanying photograph is not of Geeshie Wiley – there is no known photograph of her) and another will get you a cover by Rhiannon Giddens in 2015.

PETER RILEY

The last kind words I heared my daddy say
Lord, the last kind words I heared my daddy say

From throat to history
the message descends and is
held at a turning point
by the need *contra* greed,
turning at last to face

A war or something else
an apple in an apple tree
takes you from me
across the sea
and brings you back
in a box,
seething with animus.

If I die, if I die in the German war
I want you to send my body, send it to my mother's door

The bus arrives and picks him up.
Red light in the dark valley
extinguished at the first bend.
Salt tears moving towards the mouth,
a learned route, word by word.

To Flanders and what, after all that
merciless passion, for?
Fed half the world to death
and what next? – they
ate something or other and slept
like sparrows in a bush.

To Flanders, leaving behind
a few words, the last,
kind with no way out.

If I get killed, if I get killed, please don't bury my soul
I p'fer just leave me out, let the buzzards eat me whole

In the days of my flotation the dawn was wider,
drawn laterally to a political optimism,
or common will. The stone was
lighter over us, carved into leaf symmetries.

Dead or alive, one or the other,
we return from the wreck of that
merciless hope, the eagle's wing span
shadowing our failure, spread-
-eagled in the wind
that ruffles the sycamores,
the propellers twirling down to earth.
The power in a locked and guarded hold.

We shall bend to the task.
We shall close down Eton
and open its beautiful book
to the people.

When you see me comin' look 'cross the rich man's field
If I don't bring you flour I'll bring you bolted meal

We've all been there, we all live
the distance from here to the wall
that surrounds the sugar fields.

To unlock the darkness
any belief you can scrape off the pavement, any roughage,
bright morning star, bright despair.

I went to the depot, I looked up at the sun
Cried, some train don't come, there'll be some walkin' done

That was my hope is now my anxiety.
That was my home is now my property.
That was my comrade is now my servant.
That was my vocation is now my dying spit.
That were my songs are now my underfoot grit.
"Oh, the cradles that a man must needs be rocked in."

My mama told me, just before she died
Lord, precious daughter, don't you be so wild

That long and lonely road across the plain
she walks singing as the light dims
and the black ghosts emerge from the roadside crops.
They dance round her, they float in the air,
they dive to the plough, no more than
sketches in black ink with no
substance, no names, what are they?

Graphic voices of dead slaves.
O happy ghosts! – freed from substance,
ring-dancing around our thought, fluttering
across our sight like birthday moths.

The Mississippi river, you know it's deep and wide
I can stand right here, see my babe on the other side

But when you get to the other side of the river
there's nothing: an empty house, roof fallen,
lover fled. Promise not kept.
Small cries of distress during sleep.

The black bird sits on the cross-beam laughing
at our uncontracted employment, our unpaid labour,
our unconstituted country, our belief
that we are not, and never can be, a near-eastern war zone.

But all around the time I hear that singing.
Make me a pallet on your floor, it says and
Everything I got is done and gone and so it is,
every last remnant of my name's away.
Put out the light he sings,
if there's any light left put it out. Goodnight,
Irene and everyone. Black is an act of the eye,
whole and shared.

What you do to me baby it never gets outta me
I may not see you after I cross the deep blue sea

The sexual lyric forsaken, sailing away
into further racial hatred.
Brave boat tossed in the swell, beware
of yachts, beware of jokes, strongest of song.

You rolling river true future heart
borne away for good in a sturdy vessel
fronting the wind, sinking to the horizon –
and the wind blow high and the wind blow low –

A cargo of goodies not for us
and the cook's got the staggers
and the captain's a hog-eyed skunk
and what do you think we had for dinner?

A president's oath and a monkey's liver.
The mocking auk passes on great white wings
the moneying hawk lied without end
Old Riley boomalay. Old Riley gone away.

The world must be what it always was.
Bread and wine, fortune's edict
and the little wren up aloft
tweeting come all ye in the early light.

KELVIN CORCORAN

The last kind words I heared my daddy say
Lord, the last kind words I heared my daddy say

(Mine had nothing to say.)

The trees made new this year
are losing their leaves losing their leaves
down to their bony Beckett branches
refusing a role in a bloody drama.

The trees made new this year
mark the edge of garden and sky
and light expands where once were leaves
denying a turn in metaphysics.

If I die, if I die in the German war
I want you to send my body, send it to my mother's door

The song pushes on, the war pushes on
the war in the sky bombing the song
took the door off the hinges
lay me down on it and carry me off.

My mother's house was open then
and the world stepped in day and night
made itself at home by the fire
there's always a war, oh let me get warm.

If I get killed, if I get killed, please don't bury my soul
I p'fer just leave me out, let the buzzards eat me whole

Well wolves could do the job
and catapult my bones
I would stutter everyday
and scatter all my songs.

My own family is gone
the ground is gone and I can't fly
I've heard that word spoken
my foot halfway down the hole.

When you see me comin' look 'cross the rich man's field
If I don't bring you flour I'll bring you bolted meal

I've nothing left but a picture
of that dispossessed field
I don't recall what grew there
when you sang the old time ballad.

I'll bring you a taste of pigeon
and some comfort for your mind
but I can't cook from nothing
and make the world turn kind.

I went to the depot, I looked up at the sun
Cried, some train don't come, there'll be some walkin' done

The train called Social Mobility never reached town,
the tracks were never laid and you were barred anyway.

See my train coming? Not in this world, no I don't.
Saw the freight train leave loaded with ladders for the moon.

Imagine this as the absolutely fixed daily truth.
Even when we sing that whistle's a long way off.

The rails glint like God and all his angels
like silver lines running over the miles-away hills.

My mama told me, just before she died
Lord, precious daughter, don't you be so wild

(And she had many kind words to say.)

Don't take on so, even from love,
that wildness, it's in the world.

My mother would ask my friends
- what's going on with him?

I never knew this until after she died
And I don't even know if this relates.

Can we take on so across a world away?
I don't know, Peter this is perhaps too raw.

The Mississippi river, you know it's deep and wide
I can stand right here, see my babe on the other side

No I can't get o'er and I've no life here
the river running through all time stops me
and there you are, I can see your face
I can almost taste your skin on my mouth.

It's deep and wide and I'd take to drowning
but stand here like a poor ghost longing for Illinois
I don't even have the words to tell you this
and I see my life leaving on the other side.

What you do to me baby it never gets outta me
I may not see you after I cross the deep blue sea

Your body is a speech my love
all these years whispering in my bones
running in the blood to make it fit for joy
your body is a speech to me.

And it says – I will hold you up

against all this battering

against the charging waves

and make us fit for joy.

MICHAEL HASLAM

1. (1)

The last kind words I heared my daddy say
Lord, the last kind words I heared my daddy say

In 1965, aged eighteen and still at school, I had done well in my examinations and been accepted to read English at a Cambridge college, but with the stern advice that I should take steps to improve my French. French formed a part of the Cambridge English Tripos. I had taken Geography as an A-level, rather than French, and my O-level qualification in that subject was a poor pass. My school was the posh direct-grant grammar school, Bolton School, and it had its connections. The plan was that I should quit school a couple of months early and spend a couple of months in student accommodation at the University of Clermont-Ferrand, and a month following a course in French Literature at the Sorbonne in Paris. And this is what happened.

While I was away, my parents moved house, from a large old house in Astley Bridge, where I had grown up, to a 1920s semi in Doffcocker. These are suburbs of Bolton-le-Moors. Douglas and Jean Haslam were to occupy this house for almost forty years. For me it was not so much a home as an occasional refuge. It had a strip of garden leading down to Doffcocker Lodge. A 'lodge' in this part of Lancashire is what in Yorkshire would be called a 'dam', a reservoir made to feed a mill or a canal. The name 'Doffcocker', it was said, designated a place where millworkers would remove their clogs to cross the stream. In their garden Douglas and Jean cultivated fruit bushes and fruit trees.

Their lives came to an end in the early years of the 20th Century. Jean was suffering extreme dementia, and lodged in a home. Douglas, with motor-neurone disease, had lost not his mind but his body. By late October 2004 he was hospitalised, unable to control any muscles but those of his eyes. He could transmit messages with his eyes, by assenting to or refusing letters pointed to on an alphabet board. Shortly before his death my sisters, Jill and Pat, were at his bedside. He managed to communicate that he had something to say, and the alphabet board was produced. His message was slowly created: P-I-C-K... and with some predictive guesswork the message could be completed: "Pick the apples and plums." He died and my sisters went to harvest their father's fruit.

2.(3)i).

> *If I get killed, if I get killed, please don't bury my soul*
> *I p'fer just leave me out, let the buzzards eat me whole*

Already aged but before the dementia had set in, my mother remarked, as a joke, that her wish was, when she died, for her body to be cast on her compost heap. When she was more demented the idea was repeated, but without the humour. Of course her wish, if that is what it was, was disregarded.

On my teens, back in the 1960s, I became interested in early blues, in what is called, not entirely accurately, 'Mississippi' or 'Delta' blues. Death and burial was a common theme for the songs. Blind Lemon Jefferson asked 'one kind favour' – "please see that my grave is kept clean". The most startling, most outstanding, of these singers for me was Robert Johnson, who had a double-take on the subject. After the almost romantic line (here and in subsequent examples the first line is repeated, harmonically a fourth above):

> *You may bury my body down by the highway side*

but before the conclusion of the verse he interjects an, as it were, prose aside: "*I don't care where you bury my body when I'm dead and gone*" before concluding the verse with:

> *So my old evil spirit can catch a Greyhound bus and ride.*

In what must have been an example of living folklore the legend arose that Johnson had made a pact with the devil at a crossroads. What is the case is that he imported into his vivid imagination the idea that his music was the devil's music.

Religion has given us many vivid images, but I could never understand how burning in hell for eternity meshed with what we know of the chemistry of fire, or the textures of humanity.

ii). I arrived in the Upper Calder Valley in 1970, and I'm glad that, from the first I took an interest in a generation of old men (their wives mostly kept to their houses). This was a generation born in the early years of the 20th Century, and all dead before its close. Some I met in the taproom of the (now closed) Mount Skip Inn where they played fives-and-threes (dominoes) on sycamore tables. Once I entered and found at one table the players Percy, Nevile, Clifford, and Stanley. I made some comment about English history but it was neither understood nor appreciated. Another of my informants, up on the moor, was Jack the poacher. The moor was what he knew. Folk have been growing old ever since, but this generation was the last of its kind. Among them there was a kind of living folklore. What were probably real historical circumstances were passed on, but without regard for dates or written sources. One such rumour concerned Nelmires, a ruin on the moor-edge between two sycamore trees. This, I was told, had been a 'whisht shop', that is, an illegal distillery, a purveyor of what the Irish call poteen. But when was that? No answer. I thought it might have been connected with the flagstone delfs nearby, for quarrymen would be thirsty men, and may have been responsible for the village of Midgley having contained as many as thirteen public houses as I had heard. Even if we include the whole old township of Midgley I could locate no more than eight of them. And now there are none. Delving into 19th Century census returns I found that, mid-century, Nelmires had been occupied by a certain Josiah Crabtree, corn-miller. That seemed to fit. But I can't pass this on as 'living folklore' any more.

Once, in conversation with Jack the poacher, I seem to have declared that, when dead, I wanted to be suspended from one of the trees up at Nelmires, as food for the crows. It was a glib remark that I shouldn't have recalled having made, but it must have tickled Jack, for he kept reminding me of it thereafter.

I missed Jack's actual funeral, but it wasn't long before he died that he told me that, all his adult life he'd been paying into an insurance fund for his burial, but that lately he'd decided that he cared nothing for his interment and had stopped making payments. What difference that may have made to his funeral, I don't know. But he had previously taken an interest in such matters. He had been disgusted by the burial of H.W. Harwood, the Midgley local historian, and chronicler of the family of Harwood whitesmiths, who specialised in making brass shuttle-tips for the weaving trade. Harwood was the man who revived the Midgley Pace-Egg play in the 1930s. He was well over six feet tall, and though his coffin fitted him, the grave was too small, and the grave was filled in with the coffin at a considerable slant. Jack thought that that wasn't right at all.

3. (5) i).

I went to the depot, I looked up at the sun
Cried, some train don't come, there'll be some walking done

There seems to have arisen a legendary image of the summer of 1967 to do with Flower Power, or 'The Summer of Love'. This may not have meant much for many young people in Britain, beyond a flavour to the popular music, but there was something to the idea, and I happened to find myself on the periphery of its epicentre, around Notting Hill, in West London. A couple of my friends had been 'sent down' from Cambridge, and had moved there. Others were thinking of following them. And it was there, in W10, North Kensington, that I based myself during the Long Vacation, and it was a sort of summer of love.

I lodged myself in a flat with friends on Bassett Road, W10. The next-door flat was held by young Frenchmen, and they invited us to their party. They knew of The Beatles and The Rolling Stones, but we took with us Jimi Hendrix's 'Are You Experienced', and they appreciated that. Among their guests was Brigitte, an *au pair*, working in South Kensington. In the early hours she was fretting about getting back. I must have seemed trustworthy, as indeed I am, and someone always up for a walk, so she accepted my offer to see her to her door, which is what I did. On the way she explained that she was au pair to a certain Lady Rendlesham, who was fashion editor at Vogue magazine. There might have been a polite kiss as she turned to her basement room in a fine white house. And, a couple of days later, after agency work at a woodyard, I thought I might look her up again. That was the start of something.

Soon after we'd met, Lord and Lady Rendlesham and their children departed for their summer holidays and I moved into their au pair's basement flat. But Brigitte's father was keen for her to return to France, and sent her a ticket, London to Troyes, to pressure her to do so. She felt she had to go. I felt myself in love with her, but didn't try to stop her, and I followed her to Victoria Station with her suitcase in my hand, singing to myself Robert Johnson's song, 'Love in Vain':

I followed her to the station, her suitcase in my hand

The song concludes:

When the train left the station it had two lights on behind
The blue light was my baby and the red light was my mind
All my love in vain.

I did feel unhappy, but at the same time I was enjoying the drama of my blues, exhilarated to be living in its poetry.

That could be a sort of ending, but it wasn't quite so. Later that summer I found Brigitte again, with her family at their holiday home on the Isle of Noirmoutier, in the Bay of Biscay. I slept in a sleeping-bag in bushes by the beach. A bold dancing weasel gnawed my rucksack and stole my chocolate. One night I saw a meteorite plunge into the sea before my eyes. One morning I noticed that the Parmentier house was all shuttered up. It turned out that Brigitte's father had caught wind of the presence of whoever I might be, and had suddenly packed everyone up and returned them all to Troyes. So there I was, with no further reason to be where I was. The blues that overcame me then was not so much a Delta blues as a Celtic Twilight or Bright Atlantic blues.

ii) A couple of years before that I was a schoolboy on my way to spend time in Clermont-Ferrand, to improve my French. Passing through Paris I bought a book in French, on the forecourt of the Gare de Lyon, thinking this might be a start. It was Andre Gide's *Les Faux-Monnayeurs*. I'm not sure that I ever really understood it, but it was this, together with having read Jack Kerouac's *On the Road* that was to wreck the Geography project on the Puy-de-Dôme area that I was supposed to be doing, by agreement with Bolton School.

This paragraph is inconsequential and irrelevant except in so far as it clearly stains my memory, and has to do with trains. The train moved southwards from the Gare de Lyon. It stopped at a station, Nevers, and stayed. And stayed. My carriage filled up with soldiers, who all seemed to fall asleep. The carriage filled with flies. The train stayed where it was. I left my seat and stepped down from the train onto the platform. There I wandered up and down, until eventually there were signs that the train might be about to move. I regained my seat, and, yes, we were moving off. Looking out of my window I saw what was certainly my rucksack, plumped on the platform. That was strange. I hadn't taken it out with me. But I moved quickly. In those days you could open the doors of a moving train. I leapt down to the platform, ran back to the rucksack, picked it up and was just in time to leap up to the handle of the last carriage door as the train gathered speed. I hauled myself in and went back through the carriages to find my seat. The soldiers seemed still asleep though the flies had disappeared. As far as I could tell, no-one had noticed my little adventure. If I hadn't acted so precipitously a lost rucksack would have been the consequence. It would probably have been found, but better French might have improved my chances of reclaiming it, especially if I hadn't spotted it through the window. It was all a bit odd.

It's an image of a French taxi that convinces me that that's how I got from the station to the student block in Clermont-Ferrand. I was expected, booked in, and allotted my room.

The next day I found a note in my room that I couldn't make sense of (my French was poor). My neighbours didn't speak English, but directed me to Jim, an American *noir* on the floor above. I found him and he explained things. The note was from the cleaner and said I'd need to supply a tablecloth and wear slippers in the room. But, he said, a newspaper would do for a tablecloth, and my socks would do for slippers. I was to see a lot more of Jim. He introduced me to his friends, all very sympathetic, as the French say. At the bus station café where we'd 'hang out' (a phrase not yet much in use), Jim would sing and play guitar, a repertoire of folk blues. There was one song he'd made particularly his own. Against a guitar tattoo he'd sing:

I'm a stranger here, I'm a stranger everywhere
Honey I can't go home, for I'm a stranger there

Jim was studying medicine, but the reason he was doing this in France seemed to be that was avoiding being drafted to fight in Vietnam. He said that if he was sent he'd take his guitar and sing (pause) for the Vietcong. His song concluded:

They took my money and left me a mule to ride
Well the train it pulled out and the mule lay down and died
I'm a stranger here (&c.)

The last time I saw Jim he was despondent. He'd failed his exams and saw no alternative but to return to the United States. I didn't follow him to the station, and I don't know whether he ever got to see Vietnam.

Back in Bolton we tended to assume that we were insignificant, and that History was something that happened elsewhere, but things were happening, culturally and industrially. Culturally there was a proliferation of 'beat groups' playing mostly black rhythm and blues. Industrially there was the collapse of the cotton industry, fast or slow depending on one's timescale but prolonged by the importation of cheap labour from the Indian subcontinent. In the years to come, as I followed the tortuous progress of the Vietnam war I realised that History was what I was living in, and that most of it is in the past.

iii.) Ought else? Well, I mentioned a 'geography project'; what happened to that? I made a start on it, and went off exploring what remained if old volcanoes, and started scribbling. But my scribble soon turned into something completely different. It turned into what I was calling a 'novel' about what was happening to me in France, and girls I'd known around Bolton, Susan from Dunscar, and Wanda from Eccles, all culminating in climax or catastrophe with Nancy, an American in Paris.

In Cambridge I came to think that the structure of this writing was fine, but the style was rather naïve. I rewrote the whole thing, first in one style, then in another. This was a bit like giving myself my own Creative Writing course. Eventually it was abandoned and destroyed. It had cemented in memory some things I might otherwise have forgotten. I was still working on it, having returned to Cambridge in 1969 and living as sub-sub-tenant to the comic novelist Tom Sharpe (the intermediate sub-tenant was Denise Riley, who'd gone off, I think, to study Yeats in Ireland). I explained to Tom what I was up to, and it may have been this that gave him the idea for his novel 'The Great Pursuit' featuring a would-be writer who keeps rewriting the same novel in different styles.

How can I conclude this? Despite fierce competition for the title from media and transport technologies, I think that the twelve-bar blues was the greatest 20th Century invention, though it must acknowledge some assistance from the phonograph and nickelodeon in sundry juke joints.

ZOË SKOULDING

ANECDOTE FOR THE BIRDS

The last kind words I heared my daddy say

were not the ones about the wallpaper that he
misquoted like everyone else, and which were not
in any case the last words of Oscar Wilde. He looked
at the owl on a chain around my neck and said

it was an owl for wisdom, but I can't remember
the sound of the words, only how I understood them
as a wish, or a carving of feathers, meaning I didn't
hear them at all. Now there's only something muffled,

a bad line. When you asked about poetry and birdsong,
I mis-heard *parrot* as *parent*, guessing you meant
the give and take of words in love or imitation
that might be the same thing, my singing to you

across the sea in sounds from someone else's
throat. Oh I *heared*, yes I *heared* you. Look, there's
a buzzard. And there's a starling mimicking its cat-call.
Against the background hiss of sky it's my voice

deepening with others that won't let themselves
be buried. Just leave me out. All the same notes
and suddenly it's a different song, the birds with
open beaks and a music that would eat me whole.

TOM LOWENSTEIN

(1)

The last kind words I heared my daddy say
Lord, the last kind words I heared my daddy say

For whom did I live in that minus significance?
I assumed my father, loved so casually, to have asked me.

(2)

If I die, if I die in the German war
I want you to send my body, send it to my mother, Lord

Were we not fortunate to have been spared the thick of history?
Currents thrashing in whose shallows we picnicked.

(3)

If I get killed, if I get killed, please don't bury my soul
I p'fer just leave me out, let the buzzards eat me whole

Was I not just a spare body?
Look inside for some spiritual entity,
finding it perhaps dried as though on a coat hanger
dangled to the side of stock fish.

(4)

When you see me comin' look 'cross the rich man's field
If I don't bring you flour I'll bring you bolted meal

Did I not tell you how I might have been an object of contempt?
Still yet to eat thoroughly since that's what I'm down to.

(5)

I went to the depot, I locked up at the sun
Cried, some train don't come, there'll be some walkin' done

Listen, for example, to Dvorak, and his friendship
with locomotion.
Homesick as he stood in America.

(6)

My mama told me, just before she died
Lord, precious daughter, don't you be so wild

Forgive me. I too will gather my children.
Whether or not they required me as a mother.

(7)

The Mississippi river, you know it's deep and wide
I can stand right here, see my babe on the other side

Who remain ghosts, redundant darlings.
While I existed as an onlooker to that other's drowning.

(8)

What you do to me baby it never gets outta me
I may not see you after I cross the deep blue sea

We shall likewise be forgotten.
Nor is paper, O indifferent fathom, adequate to the translation.

KHALED HAKIM

THE BALLAD OF GEECHIE AND LV

I hear Þose desprat voises
all carrid on da wires
Þe moon ðat looks into my room
wil call me for da kill

    WIL CALL ME ꟻO A MEDISIN SHOW
    will cal me for im ill

O doctor cure my honcnes
doctor feel my teeth
& feel da scherpness of Ɜa blade
i carri in my sheeth

Out Þær in th Lone Stars
ða haers rize on my cheek
my tunge ðat stammers otherwys
now knos just how to speek

    NOW ꝪNOZ IUST HOW TO SPEK O LORD
    softly & so meek
    sayꝪing *O WO WꝴAH WO, OH WOA OOW*

I saw eyou lic a shadows paw
& cnew ðat we were ment
the anggel in my fuzzy ked
ðat told me eyu was sent
    ÐIS ANGEL SITTING AT MY SYDE
    i cnew ðat God had sent

a snarl of claws an lickerish jaws
she grips i cannot speke

& bites in-too my sorry sex
until my pips will squeek

>ONTIL I CANNOT SPEEK O LORD
>until th pips hav sqweekt
>singing *O WO WOAH WO, OH WO WO*

O Devil sons i am undon
now turn me on yr spit
da hunter haz been gutted
& da biter is now bit

>ÞE RAVAGER IS SAVIGED
>& Þe biter has been bit
>crying *OOW WO WO WAOW, OH OH WOAH*

. . .

thoze hoo ar invizibl must rite themselvs
a gost walking unseen wayz, looks for Yoo
the way yr broken wings are beeting me

a lif livd in meny wayz but rememberd for an afterthawt

but Im goona rite myself – a historie of th hart or a histrionicks of historie
– gonna rite myself into th Good Lords hand-me-down, rite myself into
a piney box

Lord, dont ask wat I can giv

>I can giv y/ th hole in my shoo,
>I can giv y/ th hole in my name,
>I can giv y/ th hole in yr daddy ware a daddy shud be
>& I gave y/ a hole in yr daddy waer a daddy shud be

So that el—O—vee, & I put this el—O—vee YEAAAARRHH!
I took this el—O—vee in a jook joint hell
all nite all day! & I ran away w/ el—O—vee one mor tyme!
so el—O—vee YAAAEAAARR! cud cume in

weele ryde a big old Ford, cleene owt yor memorie
ryde a crate of catfish to the end
a slick of dissolucion
to no end

I went to th lost & fownd to hand in my sole, & they threw me out in th
rise feeld ware a buzzard sircles a hole in a hole

    dig me a grave & bery my name
    dig me a grave & bery my blade
    dig me a trench cover me in dew
    Ile cume up sweetcorn yo chillun can chew

                . . .

O God I hope I dy bifcr th cuming Holocawst of letters

a notebook that sez Note Book, a tiny black hard book, a yelow book &
a red book, spilling into this book.

Strip all the acsidents of artifise, & leve a Godshapt mute
a Baptist wið no buttors, a mening wif no si3ne

I met da moðer of Þe wild cild, I met Þe wild moðer pregnant wið a gun
or was that th do3hter of a duppy

a do3hter of a phantom on the eestern front hoo cam bak & shewed hiz
do3ter hwat heed lernt on th eestern front –

O baby loon, I lov yu so, when yu pack yr flannel & walk owt th door, to a slip-rode in Solihul, & yu kist my fase on lonly yland in Chelmsly Wood

O babe, hwen y/ walk owt that door, w/ a 5 inch blade in yr lunchbox, pleze dont go, *DONT GOOO OOAHWO OWOAH*, Im taking ten steps closer when yoo walk owt that door

were all th occeons ink & all ða forests pens they wud never fynd yr name, at least in my lyftyme

> Yoole never kno how much yu mene –
> Ile danse a buzzard lope aronde yr spleen
> yoo wont kno yr fase in foxy eʒes
> wen ðey pick yu clene

Ile drive yor lines waer theyl never be fand, thoʒ they staar in yr fase

shud Þe world be lyf-lic still kanst thu cross Þe Sylhet *bhadʒat* to ða Chittagong hills

& wait fo Jesus to capsize da world

O rain clene th rope aronde my feet
& may yu dryve th rope into my brain
& lyk th rain may yu clene Þe rope arond myn heort

Dec 2019

IAN DUHIG

CALLS AND RESPONSES
some playlist notes for a metaphysical ballad

1 *Ain't Nothing*

So what do I know? I know diddley-squat
but squatitive negation means to say that is
the same as if I said, *I don't know diddley-*
squat but squatitive negation means to say —

that's linguistics, if not Socratic metaphysics,
possibly theology (a less-taken via negativa)
maybe maths, where two minuses are a plus,
my whole argument and appeal to your trust.

Debussy saw music as silence between notes;
absence can be its counterpoint in visual arts:
see Gonzales-Day's *Erased Lynching* photos.
The poor here get rubbed out like a bad line.

Writers and non-writers murder their darlings
but few wind up in places like Reading Gaol,
yet here our darlings may turn out murderous
and the thing we love most stick in our throats.

2 *Introducing Mrs I*

Since reading Greil Marcus on 'Last Kind Words'
I'll only hear Geeshie sing *I can stand right here,*
see my <u>face</u> *on the other side, from the other side*
not *babe.* Daphne A. Brooks agrees, saying <u>face</u>

turns the ballad into a metaphysical meditation:
self seeing itself othered in performance, but also
Geeshie's *deep communion* with her partner L.V.;
communion, a word I want to precede with *holy.*

Shall we gather at the river? Not the same twice,
face, song or river, the Mississippi I'll never see
with the misspelled Ojibwe name I had to chant
like catechism in primary school: *Mrs M, Mrs I…*

3 *Information As Material*

The Bernstein transcription of 'Last Kind Words' is shot
with dashes like Dickinson's poems or 'Tristram Shandy',
Trim's, *is a black wench to be used worse than a white?*

The Information As Material exhibition at Shandy Hall
presented Kenneth Goldsmith but when I call there now
I mainly see the immaterial, the ghost of Michael Brown.

When you see me comin' look 'cross the rich man's field...
rich men's fields round Shandy Hall draw shooting stars –
the Wold Stone landing on a farm owned by Didius' son

first broke the glass ceilings of our Ptolemaic solar system,
proving true Earth's interplanetary traffic with outer space,
so Wallace Stevens could use meteors to symbolise poems.

At a bash, he sees a poet's photo on a wall, face he can't tell,
she who'll be *surprised by queenhood in the new black sun,*
a name like rivers. He turns to us and asks, *Who's the coon?*

4 *Heavenly Bodies*
…please don't bury my soul

The Mekons thought Geeshie's playing out of this world,
not to mention how she vanished from the face of the earth
leaving no photo of her own, only six songs, a few names,
'Geeshie' (Gullah or misspelled hick insult) given by L.V. –

deliberately misspelled as 'Elvie' on their race record label
so customers would know it was a woman with that voice.
Then L.V. got Jesus, gave up their music, went to ground,
talking only of Geeshie later when pressed by McCormick.

To make sense of their sound, Mekons unwound chords,
cut lines, rearranged the dismembered limbs of their poetry
to connect the nothing there with the nothings that weren't,
the space between the verses with the space between planets

where bright stars can still be dead, a ruler of North Venus
give his name to our punk band from Leeds, Orion to Jack,
the song (maybe a misspelled O'Ryan) and Mars share his
with a bar of chocolate that helps you work, rest and play.

5 *Remains*
Pulvis et umbra sumus. —Horace, Ode 4

I believe in the resurrection of the body and life everlasting,
our Catholic priests glossed over problematic assumptions
of the physical interface, the indivisibility of the immaterial:

I asked one at school what separates souls if not dimension.
Shut up, he explained. So I bought Atlantic's 'This is Soul',
playing, singing, dancing it forever. Something understood.

…If I die in the German war I want you to send my body…
The shellac wheel pressing on their turntable could pass here
for the bronze plaques sent out after the War Office telegram.

Sometimes there'd be no bodies to follow, blown not to bits
but dust and shadows in a puff of smoke – the mirrors later
when families might be palmed off with any disjecta membra,

though that may serve as well, as a song can survive endless
reinterpretations, the taste of innumerable lips yet it remains,
a something or a nothing sweet beyond me still. *This is soul.*

6 *Dooh-Dah*

Can blue men sing the whites or are they hypocrites?
Fanon in the looking glass for baby boomer whites:
decades since I heard this song it still has me in bits.

The Irish word for human black skin's actually 'blue',
I'll have a cup of coffee while I'm taking in the news...
You'll hear Mr Bones when they play their music too,

but the US Irish got a name for backing a colour bar,
their cops for always hunting first anyone of colour:
I like to look like Nimrod when I'm riding in my car.

Scorsese's 'Gangs of New York' lies about the green,
Now it's getting near the time, I gotta make the scene,
read the book to know the truth, if you're really keen.

Can green men sing the blues the wrong men write?
Oh Lord, wish my bed wasn't silken sheets so tight...
Can lynchers' children ever sleep as easily at night?

7 *Saints and Sinners*

Gertrude Stein concluded that negroes were not suffering
from persecution, they were suffering from nothingness.
                    –The Autobiography of Alice B. Toklas

Alice at the looking glass
    sees nothing there
though L.V. and Geeshie
    stare back at her.

Now joining Alice,
    Gertrude reflects
on her new libretto
    'Four Saints in Three Acts'.

Negroes, she tells the press,
    can't tell apart
two faces in a photo...
    Life and art?

When the composer chose
    an all-black cast
their opera took off
    right through that glass

where we see all faces,
    if ours never
each side of the glass
    both of the river.

No one in these photos
    would know themselves
nor one here with no face
    the God of L.V.'s

8 *Red Letter, Black Letter, White Letter*

The Mississippi river, you know it's deep and wide…

Reading this I hear the Leeds Kop sing a Gullah air
if with new words: *The river Aire is chilly and deep,*
O-lu-wale: never trust the Leeds police, O-lu-wale.

His name we misspell to mean God Has Come Home
came to God's Own County to work but saw his face
on both sides of Aire water thanks to Leeds City Filth.

Their whitewash was a call, the first response silence,
then football chants, graffiti, songs, poetry, theatre,
Chapeltown Carnival's King David Masqueraders…

When they try to make their race an issue it is nothing.
In a chorus singing Trovatore, they are nothing. But
saying nothing, advised Dr William Carlos Williams.

Doctors were no use after Geeshie's parting Tosca kiss
made 'Skinny Leg Blues' the music of what happened,
Gonna cut your throat babe. So then she erased herself

to North Venus, maybe the Nixson grave, nix's daughter
whose records we have circled since like the solar system,
in homage, as is even this song and dance about nothing.

9 *P.S., L.V.*

I was out in the world when I made those records,
but now I don't want to talk about it snapped L.V.,
blessed with three score years and ten, unimpressed
by a nosy man with an Irish name hunting her out.

I joined the Master and gave up my music in 1937.
I hate for you to ask me now about my sinful days,
I am a member of Mount Pleasant Baptist Church
and that's the only place I do any singing anymore.

McCormick asks about the music of her childhood:
she sighs: *I don't know that those songs had a name.*
He tries reading 'Last Kind Words': *Guess it could*
have been one of my songs. Lots of them I made up.

JON THOMPSON

NAMES MADE FOR US IN ANOTHER CENTURY

For Kelvin Corcoran and Peter Riley

I

Inaudible consonants, inaudible vowels.
Call-and-response of a heart-sore world.
Something to believe in, like the simple return
of summer. Fields abuzz with agricultural amens,
a promise the world will be other than
stricken, rent by every new form of
poverty we can invent. Is that a promise
past redeeming? If we're fathers,
if we're fathers to every fallow field and
if the prayers are sung and sung again, then
maybe the last kind words will be a fidelity
to everything beaten, everything broken.
Let us believe that that is something we can still say,
let us believe that the words will say what we want them to say.

II

Forget the call to another life. The hard thing
is this one. Time's gentle suasions.
The next life, if such a thing be, can only be a
promise of tenderness. I'm thinking of the
silver sheen of light as it retreats from shore,
the old forebodings as the wind sweeps up,
across, darkening water, reminding you of what's
yours, and not. I know the words of those who
witness to denying desire, even to wasting.
Fear of the power of desire hardening into
a renunciation of desire. The fear of
naming it. Of just living with it.
Mother, the cost of making war
on it. Faith to walk through the door.

III

We say it's chance, and since it has happened, we're
absolved. Nothing in the way of the accumulation
of knowledge. What we stumble across is our life, and
the things making us us. The struggle, the real struggle,
is to not let it undo you. That self-made cell we willingly
enter. Though the intention within the larger pattern may
be pure, it may not be enough. When you look up, stars are
glittering with geometric precision. Though we might
like to believe it, we don't live out a fate determined
by them. If we have the clarity, there's always
choice, terrible though it may be. A summoning
of something beyond ourselves.
O the nameless choices that make up the soul.
The impossibility of making it whole.

IV

That work takes song to get through, song
to bid farewell to, song to get over.
Fields that go back, on, like an unacknowledged
shame. All that was thought then that could
be done was done. We still don't know
the limits of that accord. The soul doesn't want
to say that a limit once crossed over is not
going back. What happens to a country
that never asks for absolution? The song says
its heart is bolted down, and it doesn't even
know it. The land, meanwhile, in moonlight,
grows starker, lovelier, as if in recompense.
An inward loneliness moves over the field.
The stillness that accompanies a prisoner's last meal.

V

Row after row of sorrow: you
can go a hundred miles in any direction and it
won't tell you anything different. What
would it take to escape that tilled
and drilled soil? God knows the people
that run and pray. "I know, I know the people
that run and pray." God is hope and
God is despair. But the mind has to be on
distances done and undone. Old tinned-roofs
rust behind the fields. But if the fields are
flat, the mind's free. It flies
past the open land, past open air.
The old need to walk toward the sun.
The old need to leave a life undone.

VI

I don't know where these words will
find you, my daughter. I don't know if
they'll do. It's possible they'll vanish
like the reverb from a scratchy record. It's
possible the you that's you and the me that's me
are just part of history's forgotten out-take.
With words it's easy to mistake one thing
and another. And they won't tell us who
we are; only to what we're kin. But if you
hear them, you'll know them by the company
they keep. I hold no prayer but
hope for a soul that's self-healing.
Keep going past what's long since died.
Hold fast to what the world calls wild.

VII

The song wants to free you from your pain.
Not by rising above it, but by
entering into it; by touching it.
The fret in the song makes the song.
The words are not the song.
The song is surpassing the words,
even those that sing of pain.
The song says, you are going to suffer.
Everything you are, everything you
love, you will lose. You
are wandering without home. But
the song says, you can come home.
The song 's deep and wide.
A way to the other side.

VIII

You learn to speak as if you're dead.
You learn to speak with the dead.
Between the field and the tree there's
nothing to see. Just the dead
beckoning beyond the border.
It's strange the quiet in this
stubbled field. Strange to say
what you feel without words;
the old hunger to be heard, somehow.
The face you held in mind for so long is
fading. You just wanted it answering
to all the names you tried to say.
All the names that've died inside of me.
All the land taken back by the sea.

JUDITH WILLSON

LAST KIND WORDS BLUES

All the furniture in this song has been loaded onto a flatbed truck
along with chipped plates, the axe and the mattock
sheets turned sides to middle

               driven away down an empty highway
that leads only to no good god knows where
and the last gas station deserted

             then the tin-roofed house dismantled
its whole gist, joists and tiebeams
                    the crawlspace hauled up
darkness collapsing into its own weight

the unbearable distances pouring in

no bread or milk left on a table to call home the dead
who have not yet tramped back out of war
somewhere beyond blue mountains
          over a wide blue sea

but their voices have travelled before them
          they flicker *here* through dry switchgrass
here keening in the wasp nest under a wing of corrugated iron

here where the ghost of spring rain shakes a cottonwood

and a woman might turn her head as she crosses the railtracks
            coming through the scrape and grit of silica light
               carrying a sack of flour on her back

            the stove already lit

            wind blowing through her skirt

TONY BAKER

(The last kind words I heared my daddy say
Lord, the last kind words I heared my daddy say)

Put the phone down, I'll ring you back.
The garden path slopes up to where it stops
at fresh asphalt on the hill, bits of Europe
slipping off to go way, way past the tipping
point from which they might be back.

Exactly so. In some versions. A shore
of sorts that stops at nothing. Whole sentences
in which a voice goes up and over piles of stranded kelp
saying things that rush like shells, like finished articles,
completely true yet still not really sure.

And all I hear's a train-wreck of grammar
picked from the fatballs put out for the birds
wheezing their organ-grindy peeps: sing this,
talk that, think with whatever tongue you can.
Cough up. Stammer.

(If I die, if I die in the German war
I want you to send my body, send it to my mother's door

Starveling throat, get on with it, give me
something that'll sing its guts out, something

that bleats *make me hard to swallow.* Take, eat,
for this, for want of any better word's

food for thought. My weathervane,
susurrus from the ghosts that blow leaf

spume across the same old path, storming
what's left of 18 months – we don't, we can't

come in from here. The ansaphone sends back
your voice: *we're currently unavailable*

but if you'd like to leave a message…

'Steorfan' is the word I think Carl chose.

(If I get killed, if I get killed, please don't bury my soul
I pr'fer just leave me out, let the buzzards eat me whole)

A toss up between the ballpoint scrawl of stars
& those dull echoings that clap like mute wood
pigeon wings of yes yes it must be full
disclosure in this deafest month, December,

home to whatever endris night can lull it to.
What *this* is this? I'm just saying. Better frost
than a breathless pitch to force a narrative
from entrenched vowels that stumble out into

a fog of their own choosing. *Tiens tiens*, a moth
fumbling at the bedroom's toughened glass
as if it thought it knew it wanted out.
Take it, go feed the night.

(When you see me comin look cross the rich man's field
if I don't bring you flour I'll bring you bolted meal)

50 quid burns easy,
the price of a meal
for 3 at Pizza Express.

You have to laugh. *Bullion,*
I'd been saying & what
I'd meant was *Bullingdon.*

Get the bolt to the fatted
cow's head. Let's hear it
for the dead

certain ones, the rule
of the lowered down.
Let them go

then let them go with
their licorice teeth chewing
into the bargain

(I went to the depot I looked up at the sun
Cried, some train don't come, there'll be some walkin done)

Links of whiteness falling
ashes to a kind of memory blind –

Well of sense swollen well
you don't mix with such shifting

screens and live to join the dots.
The gum tree's leaves snap off

in the cold & guide themselves
to ground. Ferry me over, lil darling,

in a box or what you will,
get me to that tarred horizon

(My mama told me, just before she died
Lord, precious daughter, don't you be so wild)

Precious daughter, you with your wacky socks & nose
for charity shop woollens, who lasso Dutch talk now
with your post-bac German and skills shortage skills,
you were there, you'd know what it is that slops
up against the walls of an Amsterdam canal,
its wavelets of scuffed nouns humming unwittingly
to themselves *we're not tourists*
or low-paid migrant workers, we live here –

You'd know what it was, you were there
                                    on the slopes
above a village in Bulgaria where the cemetery
slotted into the pastures easy as a stray dog
& the walnut lady grinned at us repeating over
and over till she thought we had it
                            her word for "hedgehog"

What was it? you'd know, three – four? – syllables,
spiked and ticking in a coil like barbed wire

(The Mississippi river, you know is deep and wide
I can stand right here, see my babe on the other side)

Text us if you've a mo
let me know how it's going –
only have 2 bars

(that's telephone, not beer),
not much reception
to tell the truth.

They've been calling out
names all night but
never the right one.

Strange
but when I wrote
"us" I was meaning

no-one else: the singular
of numerousness it
seems

is still many
but becoming
less so now. Shall soon

need a visa! Please
keep in touch,
as/when.

(What you do to me baby it never gets outa me
I may not see you after I cross the deep blue sea)

And we'll stand by the shore
awaiting the outcome like the fools
we are, uncertain of being
free of the slugfest, the matchbox war

beneath the skin, tender manual showing
where every single last remaining piece
is meant to go & what this plastic implant
of a heart was ever made for

JOHN SEED

UNTITLED (1930/1939)

1

taxicab shelter Piccadilly 1934

the telephone isn't ringing

the Aerodyne Merlin radio is tuned into
no station

if I die if I die
in the German war

don't bury my soul

Bebe Daniels is 34 years old
about to retire from films
and become a radio star
but she doesn't know this yet

2

in his stifling quarters
sipping warm vodka
Tatlin

the last kind words

I heared my daddy say

singing songs of the homeless
urchins who roamed the streets of Petrograd
after the Civil War   done for
done for
done

3

Ah the pleasures of believing you

hanging on your flighty promises I'd die
willingly for one night
in your arms baby these restless
heavy nights

even if I died in disgrace
done for
drowned or something
no funeral or gravestone

what you do to me baby

who knows if there's anything up there anyway
any meaning anywhere

wars wars

send my body
send it to my mother Lord
to my mother's door

4

eye lost
where the light fades
the Mississippi river

there's no ferry
on either shore
I can stand right here

see my babe
on the other side
from the other side

5

you say you won't give it back
my heart mislaid lost gone

across the Mississippi river

what you do to me baby

it's just another spring and my heart's
gone missing

I may not see you

after I cross the deep blue sea

if somebody asks
what pleasure is there was there
sprinkling salt in an open wound

what will you say?

6

what happened
27 April 1932
to Hart Crane's topcoat
draped over his shoulders
after it was folded
neatly over the stern-rail
before he stepped off
SS Orizaba

into the Gulf
275 miles North of Havana

I may not see you
after I cross

the deep blue sea

a perfect cry

into the noon

LAURA POTTS

THE NEVER-MOTHER

Outside my skin: cold, and stone skies. I weep
and think of hands – stressed, clenched – his skull
moulded in the crack of my elbow, and rock him,

crying, caressing the soft pearls of his eyelids.
Thunder snarls in the dead of night.
Say *light* and I swallow my stomach.

He sleeps in some other arms now, my son,
wakes to the halls of dawn in another land
far from here, where a woman will not hold him

quite like I did. The moon will be old and
the stars wheeled away before I see him, my boy,
striding with limbs long to his mother's open arms;

when the skies will flame with copper, copper, crimson
and tan. When he will stop, cold, and ask me who I am.

PETER HUGHES

POEM

this evening is a stunning
range of blues from sky to
slate & back along the tracks
we've had on shuffle through
the seasons this is not our
destination even though it's
where we stop between the oak
& holly if I die say hereabouts
still swallowing the swollen pad
of an age-inappropriate sandwich
bake me clean & brush aside
this troubling flesh then tuck
my memories amongst the birch
& hazel a little smudge upon the
rain washed hawthorn just a
dusty benediction on the birch &
hazel the recent ash & beech
yes let me sleep beneath the blues
beneath the lady of the woods

Coed y Parc, mis Mawrth, 2020

CONTRIBUTOR BIOGRAPHIES

TONY BAKER moved from Derbyshire to France in 1995. He continues to live, and used to work, as a musician in the Loire valley where currently he requires no visa. He studied piano and composition at Trinity College, London, literature at Cambridge University and subsequently completed a PhD on William Carlos Williams at Durham University in 1982. Since then he has worked mainly as a musician and ecologist. He has written a book on the history of mycology and co-authored another on creative work with autistic children. In the 1980s he edited the magazine *Figs*; his most recent poetry publications are *In Transit* (Reality Street Editions, 2005), and *Three Part Invention and other scored occasions* (West House Books, 2003).

KELVIN CORCORAN lives in Brussels. He is the author of numerous books of poetry, including *New and Selected Poems*, *For the Greek Spring*, and most recently *Facing West*, 2017, all from Shearsman Books; *Not Much To Say Really* (sponsored by Medicine Unboxed, published by Shearsman Books 2017), *Article 50* (Longbarrow Press, 2018), *Below This Level*, (Shearsman Books, 2019) and *The Republic of Song* (Free Verse Editions/Parlor Press), 2020, and *Orpheus Asymmetric* (Oystercatcher Press, 2020). His work is the subject of a study edited by Professor Andy Brown, *The Poetry Occurs as Song* (Shearsman Books, 2013). He edited an account of the poetry of Lee Harwood in *Not the Full Story: Six Interviews with Lee Harwood* (Shearsman Books, 2008). He has collaborated with various musicians and composers, producing the CD, *A Thesis on the Ballad*, with The Jack Hues Quartet. Kelvin is also guest editor of *Shearsman* poetry magazine.

IAN DUHIG has written for music, usually with the Clerks and composer Christopher Fox, as well as essays, articles and short stories, but he mainly writes poetry, and has published seven books, most recently *The Blind Roadmaker* (Picador, 2016). A *New and Selected Poems* is due out from Picador later this year.

KHALED HAKIM has a background in film and linguistically innovative poetry. He took an extended absence from both, becoming a Sufi student and subsequently a Sufi musician. He has recently returned to publishing with *Letters from the Takeaway* (Shearsman Books, 2019); *The Book of*

Naseeb (Penned in the Margins, 2020); and the forthcoming *The Routines: 1983–2000* (Contraband Books).

MICHAEL HASLAM, born Bolton, Lancashire 1947, has lived near Hebden Bridge, West Yorkshire since 1970. Publications include *various ragged fringes* (Turpin, 1975); *Continual Song* (Open Township, 1986); *A Whole Bauble* (Carcanet, 1995); *The Music Laid Her Songs in Language* (Arc Publications, 2001); *A Sinner Saved by Grace* (Arc, 2005); *Mid Life* (Shearsman Books, 2007); *The Quiet Works* (Oystercatcher, 2009); *A Cure for Woodness* (Arc, 2010); *Scaplings* (Calder Valley Poetry, 2017); *Ickerbrow Trig* (Shearsman Books, 2020). Cholmondeley Award 2011.

PETER HUGHES is based in north Wales where he runs Oystercatcher Press. He also teaches and has been Judith E. Wilson Visiting Fellow in Poetry at Cambridge University. Shearsman Books published Peter's *Selected Poems* alongside a volume entitled *'An intuition of the particular': some essays on the poetry of Peter Hughes*, edited by Ian Brinton. His other poetry publications include distinctive versions of Petrarch, Cavalcanti and Leopardi. His most recent book is *A Berlin Entrainment* (Shearsman Books, 2019).

TOM LOWENSTEIN's *Filibustering in Samsara* was published by The Many Press. His other collections of poetry are from Shearsman Books: *Ancestors and Species*, *Conversation with Murasaki* and *From Culbone Wood – in Xanadu*. Shearsman will also publish his account of 1970s north Alaskan life, *The Structure of Days Out*, in 2021.

LAURA POTTS is a writer from West Yorkshire. A recipient of the Foyle Young Poets Award, her work has been published by *Aesthetica*, *The Moth* and The Poetry Business. Laura became one of the BBC's New Voices in 2017. She received a commendation from The Poetry Society in 2018 and was shortlisted for The Edward Thomas Fellowship, The Rebecca Swift Women Poets' Prize and The Bridport Prize in 2020.

PETER RILEY was born in Stockport in 1940 and recently moved to Hebden Bridge after 28 years in Cambridge. He is the author of 17 books of poetry 1967–2015, which have been gathered into a two-volume *Collected Poems* published by Shearsman Books in 2018. His long poem *Due North* was shortlisted for the Forward best collection prize in 2016.

Dawn Songs, three essays on music, was published by Shearsman Books in 2017, and Longbarrow Press has since published *Truth, Justice, and the Companionship of Owls*.

JOHN SEED is the author of around a dozen collections of verse since 1977, most recently, *Melancholy Occurrence* (Shearsman Books, 2018). His writing has appeared in several anthologies, including *A Various Art* (1987), Ian Sinclair's *London: City of Disappearances* (2006) and Neil Astley's *Land of Three Rivers: Poetry of North-East England* (2017).

ZOË SKOULDING's collections of poetry from Seren Books include *Remains of a Future City* (2008), *The Museum of Disappearing Sounds* (2013) and *Footnotes to Water* (2019), which won the Wales Book of the Year Poetry Award 2020. Her most recent collections are *The Celestial Set-Up* (Oystercatcher, 2020) and *A Revolutionary Calendar* (Shearsman Books, 2020). She received the Cholmondeley Award from the Society of Authors in 2018 and is Professor of Poetry and Creative Writing at Bangor University.

JON THOMPSON is the editor of Free Verse Editions, a book series of original poetry and translations and Illuminations, a book series on poetics. His most recent poetry collection is *Notebook of Last Things* (Shearsman Books, 2019). More on him can be found at www.jon-thompson.com

JUDITH WILLSON has worked as a teacher and in publishing. Her first collection, *Crossing the Mirror Line*, was published by Carcanet in 2017 and her second, *Fleet*, by the same publisher in 2021. She lives in the Yorkshire Pennines.

www.ingramcontent.com/pod-product-compliance
Lightning Source LLC
Chambersburg PA
CBHW031928080426
42734CB00007B/597